G
Love Poe

Melinda Morris Perrin

*For Dick & Lois,
May you grow old and foolish
together, and even more in love,
Melinda*

Ice Cube Press
North Liberty, Iowa

Goldenrods: Love Poems for the Old & Foolish

Copyright©2006 Melinda Morris Perrin

First Edition   1 3 5 7 9 8 6 4 2

Ice Cube Press
205 N Front Street
North Liberty, Iowa 52317-9302
319-626-2055 f 413.451.0223
fmi: www.icecubepress.com

ISBN 1-888160-15-2 (9781888160154)

Library of Congress Control Number: 2005925133

The paper used in this publication meets the minimum requirements of the American National Standard for Information Sciences—Permanence of Paper for Printed Library Materials, ANSI Z39.48-1992

No part of this book may be reproduced in any fashion, electronic, digital, or in any other manner without permission. Small portions may be reproduced, as in the case of a review, the publisher and author shall be provided copies.

Manufactured in the United States of America

Cover and interior photos ©2005 Melinda Morris Perrin

Dedicated to Barbara & Bob, Carol & Carl, David & Ray

And those who have love in their hearts and
see it in others, especially:
Gail & Dave
Ellie & Ed
Lisa & Stan
Linda & Jeffrey
Laura & Steve
Lee & Bob
Brenda & Morrison
Lillian & Pat
Kathy & Dan
Karen & Sam

And of course, Dan

For My Readers

Whether rediscovered with a life partner or sparked by someone new, love after 50 takes on a dimension many times more poignant than in our early years. Tragedy, illness, and loss add their own piquancy. That is what is explored in the poetry in this little book.

Most of these poems were written in the past year. They were inspired by the reawakening love between my husband and myself after he retired and suffered major Traumatic Brain Injury in a fall during a cross country move. His struggle to regain faculties, physical and mental, especially speech, is awe inspiring. Our experiences brought us closer and primed the pump, but looking around at friends and digging into the recesses of my imagination, I've drawn from many wells. The results are what I call "Love Poems for the Old & Foolish". Some are funny; some are painfully serious and revealing. All are for you.

Other new works, mainly on nature & spirituality are also included here, as well as some older favorites that fit the topic. Sometimes the line between what is nature, what is love, and what is spirituality gets blurred, as it should be.

If there is a genre called "Folk Poetry" that's where my work belongs. I am untrained and write because I am inspired or "in-Spirit". I am truly grateful that my work has been so well appreciated. The response to my first volume, *Prairie Smoke: Writings from the Heartland,* was gratifying. Many of you wrote and ordered more copies for friends. Before this I wrote for myself, now I write for you.

Melinda Morris Perrin
January 31, 2005

Table of Contents

For My Readers, 5
Invitation, 9
Love Poems for the Old & Foolish, 11
Nature & Spirituality, 63
Every Day Petitions for Muse, Friends & Future, 89
Biography, 100

Come Listen to the Land

It's the day's end.
Come listen to the land.
In the stillness of twilight,
Come listen to the land.
See the balance of dark and light.
Come listen to the land.
As shadows lengthen,
Come listen to the land.
Hear the heartbeat of the Earth.
Come listen to the land.
There's nothing more pressing.
Come listen to the land.
Together we'll sit.
Come listen to the land.
Till the cold comes to take us,
We'll listen to the land.

November 15, 2004

Love Poems for the Old & Foolish

Goldenrods

Goldenrods blaze forth
At the first hint of autumn
Bright against the browns of dying grasses
Counterpoint to rich purple asters
And clear blue skies

Love is
sweet as apples
In the autumn air
Tart and fresh and savory
Crisp and cold

Love is
Rich and full and abundant
As bright goldenrods
Shining in the sun
At the first hint of autumn

September 2004

We Walk the Sandy Land

We walk the sandy land
On an island of what once was
Adrift in a sea of what is.

Misty haze mutes
Recently revealed colors of autumn
And grey skies cloud the far-off hills.

Joy of new discovery surrounds us
Things so very old
Familiar, yet different.

You reach and pluck
A goldenrod past its prime.

October 21, 2004

Cold Morning

Cold crept into the room last night
While we lay asleep under warm blankets.
Now morning light glows golden through old-fashioned shades.
I reach for you and we snuggle,
Flannel-on-flannel sticking like children's cloth boards.
Bare toes touch.
Warmth spreads as fire ignites from the friction of our bodies.
The cold retreats to the corners and waits.

                                                            October 2004

Cirque du Soleil

The Cirque is a total experience of original music performed live, theatre, art, spectacular feats, lights, sets, wardrobe, magic, special effects, and clowns all wrapped up in a unifying storyline. My husband & I were hooked by watching a Cirque marathon on Bravo. I came up with the first verse of doggerel and after a pause, Dan came back at me with the next two lines, saving it and giving me the impetus to keep going. The result is far different from the original intent.

She: I want to run away
       To the Cirque du Soleil.
       I'll fly with style and grace
       Exotic paint upon my face.
       I'll stretch fingertip to toe
       The Cirque is where I'll go.

He: Your back you'll wrench.
       You don't speak French.

She: Well then I be a clown
       Wear spangles on my gown.
       Grin from ear to ear—
       I'll run away this year!
       They will laugh at me
       I'll be funny as can be.

He: They'll laugh all right.
       You'll be a sight!

She: I want to sing my soul
       Flying high in Montreal
       In a circle full of light
       Engaging as a sprite
       A voice so clear and loud
       I'll touch the heart of God.

He: Alas, my Dear
You're tone deaf, I fear.

She: Come run away and play
At the Cirque du Soleil.
Get up off the bench.
Come be a leetle French.
The years will disappear
As I whisper in your ear.

Won't you run away with me?
Limber and carefree we'll be.
You'll catch me as I fly
Hand to hand up in the sky.
We two will spin and twirl.
Strong boy? Pretty girl?

He: I'll run away with you
No matter what you do.
Today we'll run away
To the Cirque du Soleil.

November 2004

After the Fall

Walking down the paths of memory
You sometimes lose your way.
Trees crowd out the sunlight,
And roots rise to trip your tongue.

Still you persevere
Exploring many back roads
Taking unexpected detours
Your compass returning you
To the right direction always.

On many trips
I come too.
Holding hands
We adventure forth together.

Though the path seems unfamiliar,
The woods are less scary
In the company of love.
You point out signposts.
I give them context
For our journey.

You tell me that the path leads
To where we began.
It is a circle
That returns us to a happy place
Before the Fall.
And I believe you.
I believe in you.

October 13, 2004

Life is Good

This is a true story.

At night the sadness would start
I'd get my coat
Prepare to leave you
Alone
Lying in bed
We'd play a game
You and I
Words were hard
And so I'd prompt…

Who loves you?
You love me
And?
I love you too

After Christmas
You began to slip
Returning to the coma
That held you for so long
Retreating
Your hands began to shake
Then to curl
Hard fought gains
Gone
Horrified at what was happening
I saw panic in your eyes
And held you

Who loves you?
God loves me
I love you too

That night word went out
Across our web of friends

He needs our help

It read
By morning hundreds of voices
Rose in love
That day you couldn't sit
Tied to a chair
I'd wheel you
Along corridors
Wondering where we were going
Worry on the faces
Of your therapists
Who loved you too
Through the day
A peace descended
Panic left your eyes
That night I asked

Who loves you?
Everyone loves me
Especially me

In the days
And months
And years ahead
We'd tell the story
Of how love saved you
From the brink
Thanksgiving and blessing
Fills our days
Words sometimes fail
Frustration is never far
But today you skied

Around the yard
Dined with friends
And kissed a new grandson
Named for you
Life is good.

Who loves you?
You love me
And?
I love you too

January 30, 2005

Passing Through the Rainbow

False twilight
Changing light in a preternaturally darkened sky.
Thunder rumbles from distant Helderbergs
Heralding coming rain.

Together we walk through empty house
Remembering our brief time there.
All the shock. All the pain.
All the healing. All the love.

We close and lock the door, leaving it all behind.
We go as we came, separately, not together.
The first drops fall as we pull away.
Good-bye Hawthorn Hill.

By the road, the heavens open.
Rain falls hard and fast, matching tears finally shed.
Each car an island isolated in a vast sea.
The rain intensifies.

Manhole fountains
Plumes of spray from Earth and sky
Out of Niskayuna hills we go
Down toward the river.

By the Gateway Bridge
The setting sun appears in cloud break
Lighting the way to our new home.
Through my tears I search for rainbows.

Crossing the river,
The air is charged with crystal colors.
Passing through the rainbow
We enter western lands.

July 2004

Miracle Man

I watch you walk down tree shaded street.
I follow slowly a ways behind.
You're tired and your left foot drags a little
Giving you a shuffling gait
But you don't notice.

You are with your friend and brother
Sharing words and remembrances.
Intent on expression, you gesture,
Pleased with an audience for
Those precious words.

Once they were taken from you
Lost inaccessible
Bravely fought for
Bravely recaptured
Yours once again.

Once you were taken from us
Lost inaccessible
Bravely fought for
Bravely recaptured
Ours once again.

Our precious Love
We're pleased to walk with you.
Sharing stories. Sharing lives.
Amazed at your independence,
Our Miracle Man.

Your brother smiles
Wonder on his face.
"I never heard you sing,"
He says.
You will. You will.

January 23, 2005

Old Fool & Sweet Thang

You Old Fool
I love you with foolish pleasure.
You make me smile, wondring,
Where you've been all my life?
What kept you? Were you waiting for me
To come along and whistle in your ear?

You Sweet Thang
I was waitin for you to fatten up and ripen.
Green fruit leaves a sour taste
But woman you are just right.
You can whistle any tune you like.
I'll play your Fool.

December 18, 2004

Pictures in a Book
For Angela & Frank

A picture of a young man on a beach
Smiling at the camera
Confident and proud
Of his physique.

Hints of the man
He would become
More handsome
With a grace and wit
A camera couldn't reveal.

Another picture
A beautiful young woman
With a smile that captured hearts
And saved them for a rainy day

Hints of the woman
All grown up
And glamorous
Creating a world of beauty and grace
To grow the children

One picture today
From two lives well loved
A life well shared
Three generations of beautiful people

December 18, 2004

Memory

I take your feathery-soft hand in mine
And see the girl you were
High-stepping in the tall grasses of the meadow
Bouquets of flowers in your arms,
Sunlight streaming through your copper hair
A wayward lock blowing in the summer breeze.
I tell you of my memory and see the doubt creep in your eyes.
"You're lovely still," I finish.

You smile and say, "I remember that day...
And a lanky boy with a slow smile
Cocksure and full of himself
Sitting on the stone wall that marked the field
Watching me pass.
Was that you?"

November 14, 2004

Teenagers in June

Chipmunks chase across concrete.
More speed than sense
They plunge in deep blue water.
Frantic ripples signal their distress.
I fish them out with net I keep
Just for that purpose.
"Better alive than other," I think.
They lie panting on green grass
Then, continue chase.

Six jays land in the yard.
Beleaguered parents hounded by fledglings
Old enough to fend for selves.
Young ones angrily demand food
With open beaks and raucous cries.
"Teen years are nature's way of saying
It's time to leave the nest," you observe.

July 2004

The Time to Live is Now

In the warmth of the summer night
We lay together
separate yet companionable.
I smell the rain through open window.
The sound of crickets fills the air
Carried on a gentle breeze.
A clock chimes the half hour
And you begin to snore softly.

Our love is as sweet as the late summer night
And as full as promise paid.
I wonder at the miracle that keeps us together
Forty years and more.
Who will be the first to leave
And what of the one left behind?
But these are questions for another season
The time to live is now.

August 2004

Windshield Time

Oh to be alone with you
Only a windshield
Between us and the future
Sharing tomorrows that never arrive
Sharing yesterdays that never end

Miles pass by
Hours on the road
Filled with stories, songs, and laughter
The flow of words stimulates ideas
Creative juices make us thirsty

Outside the landscape slowly changes
We see but are untouched
By rivers, land and sky
Isolated by the windshield
We travel well together

December 11, 2004

The Magic of the Night Blooming Gourd Plants

A porch light illumines deep darkness
Casting shadows among gourd vines.
Warm night air hangs heavy with pungent smell of
	sweating plants.
Ruffly white flowers glow luminescent in weak light.
Overhead leaves of trees rustle in the wind
Speaking of approaching storm, still miles away.

I walk among the vines that canopy the garden
Encouraging them to be strong,
Whispering to fuzzy baby gourds,
"Hang on. Grow big."

Shoots of new growth reach out over the path,
Demanding attention and support.
I pet furry big elephant ear leaves,
Caressing them between my palms,
Loving their softness.

I can feel the hunger of the plants,
Like hunger of a woman in the late stages of pregnancy.
Roots seek nourishment and water from the rich soil of
	the Earth.
Strong tendrils, like fingers and hands, seek support to pull
	themselves up.
Heavy, pregnant wombs fight to give birth to new life.

There is sensuality in the blooming male and female flowers
this autumn night.
I can smell their musk in the heat and humidity.
There is a rich depth to their sexuality
That wasn't there earlier in the season.
It speaks of their maturity and awareness of all life's stages.

I dip my finger into male flower and feel the feathery dryness
    of the pollen.
Carefully I carry it to female flower six inches away.
By contrast, female receptors are swollen and aroused.
I gently rub my finger against them.
They grow moist with touch, and slippery.

On the other side are more female flowers.
A few males poke their heads through the fence for one
    night's bloom.
I repeat the process, picking up pollen dust on fingertip,
Spreading it against hard pistils of female flowers
Growing wet with stimulation.
Each time I marvel at the experience of union, conception,
    and birth.
Magic is in the night.

September 1997

Reunion

Under the eaves of a garret in Germany
I listen
Sounds of lovers in the room beneath
Warm my heart.
I hear them talk
Lying together in the early morning light.
When young
Their passions burst forth in the frenzy of war.
Now reunited
They delight in each others bodies.
Sweetly
They note the changes
And thank the fates that brought them
Together again.

Will that be us
I wonder?
I love the thought
That we find one another
Years hence.
Will time be kind
And give us this pleasure?

September 2004

Bittersweet

Bittersweet is the gift of autumn.
The blazing-forth of the hard berry,
Bright against twisted, dried stalks.

Bittersweet holds bitter-truth,
All the more poignant
Against the certainty of coming snows.

Its orange a brilliant blend.
Yellow for the love within the heart,
Red for the fire, which burns hottest
Before it's extinguished forever.

Framed in stiff, dried petals,
Each berry divides in four,
A kernel of knowledge
For each stage of the cycle.

Through tears of awareness,
I hang it on my door,
Grateful for bittersweet lessons
Reminders of the autumn of life.

November 21, 1998

This is the Season

This is the season for long reflective walks
For roads not taken
For things that might have been
For remembering the way things were
And will never be again.

This is the season for remembering
Friends long gone
Friends who are leaving
And friends whose parting
Is still a fresh wound on our hearts.

This is the season of radical changes
In the weather
In our lives
As children grow
Leaving us behind.

This is the season for letting go
Facing new challenges
Closing chapters
Opening doors.

1992

Empty Garden

The garden's empty now
Except for roots left
To sustain us through the winter.
The leafy red stalks of beets
Still support greens nibbled by insects.

In the early morning fog from the river
Deer graze,
Brazen in their claiming of leftover harvest.

Pumpkins still green
Will not ripen in time for Halloween
And so are left by the farmer
Who has no use for them.

In the shallow heat of noonday
Migrating birds
Stock up for the long night's flight.

Many colored zinnias give false cheer.
In solitude, a lonely Sunflower
Droops its head,
Seeds left as an offering
To those who will be grateful for the gift.

In slanting rays of late afternoon sun
Glowing golden across the fruitful land
We walk together
Not yet stewards, but observers of this place we love.

October 13, 2004

The Playground

The playground at the edge of the woods lies empty.
No shouts of children ring out in the cold, crisp air.
Once their songs echoed down the valley.
Where did they go?
Will they return?
Will a new generation discover the wonders
Of swings and jungle gyms empty and waiting?

October 13, 2004

Backwater

Grey light cannot penetrate the fog of cold air and warm water
As the canoe glides silently in the still waters of the
      morning river.
Paddles dip, and strokes are long and smooth
As we pass between island and shore.
Day breaks
Touching the golden tops of trees with light.
But still the silent stillness surrounds us like a prayer.
Ahead is the main channel and we see the ripples of
      faster current.
Our sojourn in the backwaters is ending.
Sadly we push on.

                                        October 13, 2004

The Boy Next Door

The idea for this poem came from my neighbor, Judy, whose second husband was her childhood sweetheart. I thought I'd draw upon my own experiences to flesh it out, but got caught up in all my own memories. The original intent was to bring the two together later in life like my neighbors, but it got too personal, so left it here. It's dedicated to Craig and our childhood together in innocent times.

We were three
When we first met.
You knocked me over
Pulled my hair
And made me cry.

All was forgiven
When we were ten.
We rode our bikes,
Under summer sun.
Swam together,
Splashing in clean blue water.
Your yellow hair was cut in crew
To keep you cool.
Likewise, my long black page boy gave way to
Something called a pixie.
I played the violin
And saw the look of amazement in your eyes.
You taught me to pitch a softball,
Got mad when I struck you out.
That year, you'd walk me home from school
Occasionally carrying my books
But more often pelting me with snowballs
Throwing snow down my boots
To make me cry.

At twelve we shared love's first kiss
Roller-skated in circles hand in hand
At the Junior High.
We talked for length on the phone
Looking at each other through facing windows.
I wore your picture in a locket round my neck
And a ring with a pearl your Mom got in Japan.
That summer you broke my heart
And made me cry.

You redeemed yourself the next
When Johnny, Elvis to your Pat Boone,
Stood me up.
You stayed with me and dried my tears
Missing a game you were to pitch,
And your team lost.
We danced together at Fortnightly School
Learning jitterbug and foxtrot.
Outside you threw bubblegum
That landed in my hair
And made me cry.

Freshman year you broke your leg in football,
But made the down.
I took you school work, bubblegum,
And made you laugh though
Embarrassed at your pajamas.
Outside the hospital, I cried at your pain
But you never knew.

That year your Dad was transferred
And you moved away.
I watched the trucks
Roll away down Elm-lined street
And cried.

In coming years visits were frequent,
My family staying with yours in Maryland.
Bedrooms and pajamas no longer embarrassed us
Though friendship never faltered into deeper realms.
Summers you'd stay with us, dating my best friend,
We'd double to the County Fair
And keep each others secrets.
I called you when I got engaged.
Gentleman you were, you wished me well
And broke down as you said,
"I thought it'd be me."
That was not to be
But still I cried.

January 26, 2005

Joe Pye

Joe Pye, also called Joe Pye Weed (Eupatorium maculatum), is a plant native to North America. In bloom it is an explosion of pink flowers atop a tall stem with whorled leaves. Folklore tradition says it was named after a Native Medicine Man who used this healing plant exclusively. The spirit of Joe Pye Weed appears to me as a Sam Shepard cowboy. That's my Joe Pye.

Fireworks
In night black sky
John Phillip Souza
Fourth of July
My Joe Pye

Tall and lanky
Long and lean
In cowboy boots
And tight jeans
My Joe Pye

Rodeos and
County fair
Happy-go-lucky
Without care
My Joe Pye

Cotton Candy
Swirled on a stick
Stroll down the Midway
With rides and tricks
My Joe Pye

A warm afternoon
Swaying hammock swing
Rock n Roll
A dance in spring

My Joe Pye
Checkered tablecloth
Picnic afternoon
Cakes and treats
Ears of corn
My Joe Pye

Stories shared
Around a fire
A private laugh
A fantasy lover
My Joe Pye

January 26, 2005

The Two Are One

As shadows shape the things we see,
To know the light,
We must experience the dark.
The two are one.

Discord makes sweeter harmony
The highs defined
By lows in life and song.
The two are one.

Textures and patterns intertwine
Future and past
Follow as night and day.
The two are one.

One voice cannot sing harmony,
But one and one
Combine to make a blend.
And two are one.

Your voice then compliments my own
Giving mine shape
In pitch and tone. Together we
Become as one.

June 26, 1993

Joe

Walking down the street
I saw you half a block ahead.
My heart and pace quickened
For just a moment.

Your name was on my lips
As I thought, "Wait up!"
Then I remembered
You are gone.

This man was so like you
Your height, your build
Your hair, your walk.
I miss you, Joe.

You are with me still
So close and yet so far
Not of this Earth, but
A breath away.

I stood and watched him
Catch the light
And hurry on ahead
Leaving me behind.

See you soon, old friend.

2002

That Love May Grow

That I may hear your words
Listen to mine.
That I may know your heart,
Speak to mine.
That I may follow your dreams,
Share mine.
That I may grow in love,
Grow with mine.
That I may share your life,
Give me time.

April 1996

Thirty-Three Years

You are so far away
I have to shout to be heard
But I can't breathe
Because there isn't any air.

When did you stop loving me, I cry
I do love you, you reply
Then when did I stop
Being able to feel your love.

The shortest distance between two points
Is a straight line
If both are facing
One another.

Please turn around
And so will I.

August 1998

Don't Touch!

Don't touch!
Or if you do,
Be gentle.
My rough thick bark
Has been stripped away
And I am as tender
As a new-born babe.
A cut would fester, scab and scar.
A bruise would bleed and blacken.

Take care!
This smooth, thin membrane
Is very fine.
A soft caress would feel so sweet,
But an unkind word would scratch and mar
This delicate veneer.
Oil would be very soothing,
And protect my new-found openness.
Treated right, I may develop a patina
Glorious and glowing,
Lustrous as a precious pearl,
For you alone.

April 1996

Lying Alone

Lying alone
I think of you
Missing your touch
The caress of your eyes

In my mind
You are with me
I can almost smell
Your sweet skin

Feel the weight
Of your body
Next to mine
In the dark

A warm flush
Surrounds me
The ache dims
But not the yearning

Awakened now
And lying alone

1998

Touch Me

Touch is an art
That gets better with practice
Isolation leads to alienation
And you lose your touch

Life without touch
Has no art
Life without art
Has no meaning

Touch me
So I can breathe
Touch me
So I can feel
Touch me
So I can cry
Touch me
So I can live again
Touch me.

1996

Sea Song

My body holds the waters of life
Salty and fresh my spray
My soul is wide and deep as the deepest sea
Moving, ever moving
Flowing, ever flowing

I respond to the rhythms of the tides
I undulate as the waves roll to shore
I feel the power within me
Coming from the darkest night
Riding, riding
Riding the crest
Holding my breath
As it breaks the surface
Then gasping for air
I lay back and enjoy the rush
Then wait for the next set
To carry me along

                                                          July 1997

The Gift of Less

We grow older
Responsibilities diminish
The need to acquire to sustain fades away
Lives become simpler
Homes are in order
Rhythms slow
Stripped of externals
Patterns become less complex and busy
The design of our lives becomes clearer, more elegant
Relieved of the burdens of child-bearing and child-rearing
Physical bodies return to a simpler state
No longer driven by the need to procreate
Passions deepen
A level of intimacy hard to comprehend by the young
Is discovered
Sensuality grows between caring couples
No longer trapped by out-of-control raging hormones

Choices crystallize
Privacy and space increase
We have the time to feel and explore

What we lose in acuity of hearing
We gain in inward listening
We have the time for self-knowledge

What we lose in outward speed
We gain in inner knowing
We have the time to process

What we lose in physical sight
We gain in insight
We have the time to reflect

What we lose in physical attachments
We gain in enriched inner ones
We have the experience to comprehend life's patterns

Aging well requires a shift in focus
This shift is a process, a long difficult one
But rewards are great for those who successfully
Accept, adapt, and appreciate the transition
Calmness comes
Grace descends like a comforting blanket
We become a refuge for those ravaged by stresses and strains
    of life
But only if we ourselves let go with love and dignity

Each stage of life requires a shift in perception
Each is marked by a signpost, followed by a journey to the
    next destination
Each step builds on past learning and growing
Birth followed by childhood
Maidenhood and manhood
Union with a partner
Followed by parenthood
Finally the Wisdom Years
The time to learn the meaning of life
To pass along what has been gained
Before the finality of death
The promise of new beginnings

                                                    January 1999

For Terri

Terri lies
Locked in a body that cannot sustain itself
But buries a captive soul

Day after day
Year after year

Is life the prison of unknowing consciousness?

Life is awareness
Self sustaining and free
Free to make choices

Free to live
Free to die

Is love the shackles of tubes and monitors?

Love is letting go
With peace and dignity
Acceptance and love

Being there
Holding the hand

March 28, 2005

Terri's Plea

Do you love me?
I want you with me.
Do you love me?
You cannot leave.
Do you love me?
Stay here.
Do you love me?
Yes
Then release me
I cannot.
Release me to the arms of God.

March 28, 2005

Ermine Ice

I watch as the river slowly disappears
under a mantle of ermine ice.
Yesterday a thin sheet of clear broke apart.
Seedling ice flows joined fellows downstream.
Overnight wintry winds blew cold.
Ice flows united once again
thicker now, topped with snow.

But dark pools of water still remain
To remind of days running free.
In the grey dawn
Even these pools begin to freeze.
I didn't know
my river would go
from sight.

Like all of us
it remains wild within.
Only stiffer, stiller
in preparation for the cold dark winter.
Under my gaze, ripples deny the inevitable.
The crusty cover breaks from shore.
Ice slides slowly downstream.
The river moves again!

O let my soul defy death's end!
Break through
Wild and free
Like my river.

December 20, 2004

White Mist of Winter

White winter mist
Obscures the road ahead
And closes in behind

Isolated on my journey
I follow the path of present
Adrift in place and time

Is the future up ahead
Or past remembrances
I cannot tell

I climb the hill
The mist is brighter
Still, no sun

Sheer curtains surround my world
Cloud my vision
What to do

Keep on going
Spiraling inward till
I disappear

January 14, 2005

May Our Hearth be a Haven

I try so hard.
But why?
Love is there.
Peace comes in stillness.
And yet,
I struggle.

I yearn for simplicity.
I'm happier with focus.
I do so much
That takes me away from you,
The source of my happiness.
But why?

Winter is a time for a return to basics:
For going within
Shedding extraneous thought
Shedding extraneous events
Cleaning the house of the soul

Solstice is the time of nurture
A time for family
Telling stories
Sharing laughter
Feeding one another
In body and soul.

Though the winds may howl
Outside our door
Together we keep
The fires of love and ideas alive
Inside
Giving them the breath of intention.

May our hearth be a haven
For those seeking comfort
For those seeking rest
Friendship and family.
May the warmth of our love
Radiate as the sun
Driving the cold and dark away.

              December 17, 2004

The Season of Peace

The peace of the season
descends like fluffy white flakes of snow
falling outside our window.
We're ready.

Time now to take a breath
think about why we're here
what has happened.
Time now to enjoy what we have together.

Opportunities to make a difference
in the world
in other lives
will come again I know.

Our deeds will ripple out,
across the waters of life
but for now, let it start
with a small snowflake falling from the sky
touching our loved ones with peace.

December 6, 2004

Go In Peace

> Dedicated to Marilla Thurston Missbach

It is not death I fear but dying,
That long, slow decline of body and mind
trapping the essence that is me within.
How lucky those that do not linger,
but finish up their work quickly and are gone.

I am not brave.
I do not want to watch my friends and loved ones travel onward,
leaving me behind to mourn not their passing, but my loss.
I am not brave.
I fear pain and suffering even more
and the numbing, dumbing effect of drugs most.

Yet, how wonderful to see the garden that is my life
Pass through its seasons—all of them.
Savoring each one fully and denying none.

The springtime planning and plowing
Knowing that the seeds that I and others planted are
Drinking in the rain, gaining nourishment from the rich earth
Receiving inspiration from the warming sun.
Growing, ever growing, throughout the summer.

Protecting my garden from those things that would destroy it.
Weeding out the things that are not needed.
Replanting with new ideas and experiences.
Finally, giving up my bounty for the benefit of others.
The joy of sharing, of loving,
Knowing that as I am consumed, I become one with
    the Universe.

That is the time to go
Not the time of bud,
Not the time of full-flower
But the time of joyful letting go.

And yet, there comes a time when the field is at rest, that
    fallow time,
When one reflects upon the circle of the seasons of life
And sees with clear eye what has been done, and what has been
    left undone.
Perhaps after all, that winter is the time of letting go.

If that is so, let me go in grace
With a contented heart that comforts those I leave behind.
Let my mind be strong, my spirit pure,
    and my life inspire those who are touched by it.
Then will I go in peace.

December 1995

Soul Travel

My soul sails in a boat
My soul floats on a moat

My soul is on the ground
My soul goes round and round

My soul is like the rest
My soul goes east to west

And when my soul is through
My soul flies up to you

April 29, 2004

Nature & Spirituality

Crystal Teardrop

Crystal teardrop in my window
Refracts light in rainbow hue.
The only color in a scene of
Water-paint snow, but is that true?
The snow has color too.

Each flake sends forth
Cyan, green, and violet bright
Gold, indigo, and magenta light
Red-orange and yellow till
In confusion, our eyes distill
Them all as white as snow
Agleam in sun of winter's glow.

A teardrop is all my eye divines
In the simplistic nature of my kind.
Great Mystery is not mine to see
Nor yet the multifaceted face of Thee.
It is all as white as snow
Beyond the teardrop in my window.

January 8, 2005

Star Dance

Stars dance widdershins in southern spheres
Unwind the sacred spiral of the year
Gold and white in circles round
To music without sound.

Clothed in mystery of velvet skies
Venus, star of love, arise!

While northern climes enhance
The circle of a sunward dance.
Tighter the rounds in night embrace
The glory of an inward pace.

But still the two are equal met
The balance of a well matched set.

Which way to dance when at the middle?
Do they waver just a little?
Two steps one way, then the other
Do they search for distant lover?

Oh, to hear with heaven's ears
The music of celestial spheres!

January 8, 2005

On Hawthorn Hill

Tree reflections dance in wind-stirred waters.
Verdigris chimes gently sing bulbs awake.
Colors brown and grey are gentle on the eye.
Spring comes slowly to the woods on Hawthorn Hill.

Heat hangs heavy in the air, releasing the smell of kitchen herbs.
A wind picks up and tree leaves show their underskirts.
Flies bite. Far off thunder heralds welcome rain.
Summer's in full bloom on Hawthorn Hill.

Pine needles are the first to drop, covering the earth with
    brown, sappy blanket.
Soon summer green retreats, revealing the hidden colors of
    leafy treetops.
The setting sun glows golden on the yellow Sugar and
    Crimson Maples.
Autumn paints its colors on Hawthorn Hill.

The snow lies deep on the lee side of the hill.
In the night, Pines crack and split under the weight of
    snow-laden branches.
The moon casts long shadows across the frozen pond.
Winter's white stays long on Hawthorn Hill.

                                        April 2004

The River Runs to Greet the Sun

The rising sun reflects upon the waters
The river runs to meet it.
I watch mist rise in bitter air.
Pushed by gentle breeze,
It races faster than the current.

The sky rains yellow leaves.
A light coat of frost covers the land.
The earth is at rest,
But I'm awake,
Eager to greet a new day on the old land.

Across the water,
An island holds promise of new discoveries
To those who will brave the wet.
Dry and warm in my little room,
I think, "Another day."

November 5, 2004

Earth Prepares for the Solstice

Sheets of thin ice float down the river this frosty
        December morning
Seedlings of the behemoths that land on the garden in spring
Looking all the world like beached white whales

The Canadians are gone from their brief rest on the shore
They arrived two days ago in a noisy honking horde
But were good neighbors on their visit
Finishing up the grain and vegetables left for them by the farmer

Across the water a ribbon of snow hugs the shore
And the banks of the island are cold with frost.
Gone are the mosquitoes of summer
Gone are the golden leaves of autumn
The Earth prepares for the Solstice.

                                                December 18, 2004

At the Edge of a Pine Woods

Snow started falling yesterday morn
Continued through the day and all this past night.
Will winter never end?
Where is the sun to break apart these thick grey clouds?
O, where are my signs of spring?
I stand at the window, hands round a cup, and watch the birds.

Five Robins were my Valentines,
Pushed north by slow-moving storms.
Mighty early I thought.
By the Equinox they still huddled
In the warm oasis of the dryer vent.

Goldfinches' bright-yellow summer plumage
Begins to peek through dull winter buff.
Six at a time, they perch at the thistle feeder.
Others content themselves with sunflower seeds until a
    berth opens up.
A flash of yellow marks their flight across the yard.

I watch the Cardinal couple wait in the Wahoo
Seeking sunflower seeds dropped by Chickadees.
The crimson male is bright against green foliage.
His elegant mate appears larger now,
Or is it just me who anticipates the babies of spring?

Migrating ducks make awkward passage in the sky overhead.
Small wings flap hard to keep short squat bodies aloft
In comparison, the royal Canadians seem so effortless.
The ice on the Mohawk has broken,
Maybe they will visit for a while.

I begin to be blasé about another foot of snow.
How long can it last?
Maybe I'll bundle up, go down to the river and see the ducks.
Maybe I'll ski out my door.
I like living on a hill at the edge of a Pine Woods.

March 2004

Winter Images

White snow
Red fox
In the yard
A Christmas card

Crystal woods
White deer
A happy omen
This New Year

January 8, 2005

Robins

Ten below with bitter wind
Winter storms from west and south collide
Straight ahead in little tree
An unexpected flock of early robins
Wish for warmer days.

February 21, 2004

Punxatauney

Somewhere deep in Pennsylvania
Groundhog wakes from dreams of summer.
Pokes his head out from his hole and
Sniffs the air.

A sudden blast of cold,
The cheer of crowds and
Blinding light of TV crews
Startles this solitary creature.

Quickly he retreats.
Snuggling down once again in his cozy den
He dreams of meadows with pretty flowers and succulent roots,
Warm sunny days and gentle rains.

He leaves the icy blasts
To the noisy, nosy two-leggeds
Puzzled at his reticence to be a prophet.

February 21, 2004

The Day Dawned Red Behind Blue Hills

The day dawned red behind blue hills
And March blew in on lamb-soft clouds.
Above our heads they play,
Kicking up their heels
On breezes we see but do not feel.

The deep snow retreats by inches
Revealing winter's debris.
Under the finch feeder
A little mouse nose peeks out a hole
In a ice-formed pile of thistle hulls
That holds the pattern of his journeys.

A tom turkey proudly
Escorts his harem out of the woods
Across the yard of wind burned buff duff.
The hens eye the emerging spring green as
His lieutenants flank the flock keeping order.

The cold is with us still
But there is promise in
The day dawned red behind blue hills.

March 2004

The River Flows

Good Friday dawns.
Jagged thick blocks of ice
Clog the river shore to shore.
They begin to move.
I know it's so though I can't see it.
The inner movement undiscerned
Imperceptible
But there none-the-less.
The landscape changed overnight
And some unseen force
Drives the edges of the craggy mass
High upon the bank.
Elsewhere
Channels of the river are clear
But here
Between land and island
A red fox skips across frozen water.

Easter dawns.
The river is free once more!
Free from the frozen prison
That held it through long dark winter nights.
The promise of return fulfilled
It flows
Unconcerned
By my watchful vigil.
The undercurrent was always there.
To be a river
It does not need me to believe.

March 28, 2005

Cold March Rain

The cold March rain
Falls hard upon the earth
Turning live landscape to shades of grey.
The veil of water erases all edges creating
A black and white movie without contrast.

The concrete-colored river runs again
Banked by mounds of dirty snow and ice.
Clay-colored puddles reflect dull skies
As ripples overlap in diffuse patterns.

Orange fireplace flames reflect in the window.
I feel the heat on my flannel-covered back
And wait for the room to warm.
My hands cup round my steaming morning mug.

The sun, higher now,
Begins to burn away the rain-soaked clouds.
I watch as grass begins to green in yellow light.
The world comes into focus.

March 28, 2005

The Anger of Spring

Rain pours down on frozen land
Day after day on frozen land.
Rivulets of water, rejected by ice-hard earth
Rush across the frozen land.

Denied a welcoming embrace
The water cuts paths as jagged as fire in the sky.
Scouring earth like a rejected lover
It picks up detritus of man and nature
And carries it along.

Tributaries swell.
Once quiet streams roar with anger
Turn on banks that once contained them
Run down ancient rock strewn hills
Pushing all in their path to the river below.

In the valleys
Where the rivers flow in steady current day after day
Meandering through meadows and fields
Waters rise and pick up speed.

Islands disappear under spreading waters.
Trees appear rooted in midstream.
Roots are ripped from tenuous hold
To the Mother that bore them.
Unable to withstand the force
Trees tumble and are carried along.

Lowlands flood.
Muddy waters overrun barriers
Eddy back and fill in hollows
And still the waters rise.

Sometime in the dark of night
The river crests and falls.
All the next day the waters recede
Leaving mud-covered, debris strewn fields
And trapped pools of water where geese swim.
Overhead carrion birds circle
Searching for treasure of unfortunates.

For days the current flows fast and furious
Like a lover remembering early hurts and slights
But no one stays mad forever
And through mud left as a peace offering
Green plants begin to show.

April 20, 2005

After the Flood

Flood waters recede
Rich brown mud
Covers the land
A study in sepia
In the warming days
Textures and shadow delineate
A monochromatic world
The bark of bare trees
The flowing river
The scoured earth on the island
All are equal
All the same
In early April
After the flood

April 20, 2005

Gifts from the Grandfathers

Thundering Grandfathers
Ride in from the west
Mounted on rain-black clouds
That blot the late day sky.

From the hill
We watch them come.
Loud and fierce they are,
Full of bluster and wind.

Rain pours down,
Bolts of lightning all around.
Finally bright streaks of sunlight
Mark their passing.

We smile and
Rush to eastern door
Eager to discover rainbows
Left behind as parting gifts.

June 2004

Great Egret

Out my window
Framed by a pine
Framed by panes of glass
A Great Egret fishes
In the waters of the Mohawk

Long white neck
Gracefully keeps time
To music I cannot hear as
Long black legs
Step carefully
In still waters
Off green Oneida Island

I watch his dance
Slow and deliberate
Head bobs suddenly
Fastidiously he picks and
Long beak comes up empty

Majestically he spreads
Long white wings
Lifts off to settle further upstream
Where fish are not so wary

Is he a wanderer
Seeking sustenance on his journey
Or has he fished these waters all summer
Unobserved
A rare sight
Either way

I wish to be his companion
This beautiful September day

In the sunshine
On the river
Wading in the cool shallows
Off the Oneida
Instead of prisoner
Writing these lines
Framed behind panes of glass

                                                September 17, 2004

Goldenrods in Summer Breeze

Chatty in the summer breeze
Goldenrods share secrets with the trees.
Bright against the clear blue sky
They wave at dragonflies passing by.
With Purple Asters they will joke
Like ordinary, common folk.
To Monarchs, Goldenrods will bow
And give a leg to Lady Cow.
They harmonize the whole day long
With Sunflower's loud cheerful song.
But when your heart is full of tears
The Goldenrods are all ears.
And when the evening breeze does die
They finally will close their eye.

January 26, 2005

The Village

In the mist of morning
I see the villagers
Women and children and dogs
Working in the fields
Bringing in the harvest

At the edge of the woods
On higher ground
Is the image of the longhouse
Smoke rising from its roof
Men raise up baskets of bark to make the home secure
Boys chink walls with mud from the riverbank

Old Ones sit outside by the fire
Blankets wrapped round their shoulders
Passing pipes and telling stories
Of earlier times
In this place by the river
Where the Three Sisters grow

The weak sun warms the late fall air
And they are gone from sight

October 13, 2004

Death comes to the Rookery

This poem is based on the linking of two occurrences. There was a large Crow rookery of long-standing in Evanston, Illinois. During the virulent Midwest West Nile Virus in 2000 that killed many crows, the rookery, to the dismay of residents, disappeared suddenly. A few months later, less tolerant citizens of Troy, New York were up in arms over a large crow rookery that had suddenly appeared in their neighborhood. I like to think the social crows had migrated.

Death comes to the Rookery
On the shores of Lake Michigan
Crows by the hundreds
Drop from the tree.

The Wheel of the World turns.
Death. Death. Death.
They whisper,
This place is death.

Touching the Earth
With hops and flapping wings
The Wise Ones Council
The Edict is heard.

The Wheel of the World turns.
Leave. Leave. Leave.
They whisper
This place is death.

In grey morning light
The Rookery is bare.
The Keepers of Earth Law
Have fled this space.

The Wheel of the World turns.
Fly. Fly. Fly.
They whisper.

This place is death.

The Wheel of the World turns
Life is the promise
On the shores of the Hudson
A large Rookery appears.

The Wheel of the World turns.
Life. Life. Life.
They whisper.
This place is life.

November 27, 2004

Every Day Petitions
For Muse, Friends & Future

Ode to Sleep or Insomniac

I yawn
To signal sleep
Snuggle deep in nest
Of pillow, blanket, sheet
And still she doesn't come.

I sigh
Relax myself
From skull to toe
And wait with open mind
For sleep to catch me unawares.

I wait
Hopeful
Warm and tired
For that sweet rest
Hopeful, warm, tired, waiting…

Click.
I give up.
On goes light
My glasses too,
I pick up pen and write.

April 9, 2004

A Sunday Writer's Petition

Sun Day
Ra Day
God of the Sun
Ride Your chariot
Across the sky

Giver of Light
I worship you
I honor you
Come to me and warm my soul
Through words divine

                                                        August 15, 2004

"Be As Frodo"

My friend, Stan, used to encourage his wife to "Be like Frodo". It is such sage advice, especially to those who, like the young Hobbit in *Lord of the Rings*, are just starting off on their life adventure.

Be as Frodo.
Never take for granted all the comforts of the Shire.
Respect your Elders and care for them.
Know the worth of close friends.

Be as Frodo.
Have a pure heart.
Accept adventure as it comes.
Make new friends.

Be as Frodo.
See the good in others.
Love the unlovable.
Trust your instincts.

Be as Frodo.
Know your path.
Though the way is long and hard, persevere.
Accept the help of friends.

Be as Frodo.
Be unselfish.
Work for the good.
Be a good friend.

Be as Frodo.
Know that you may have to go on alone.
When there is no hope, believe in yourself.
Fight against evil.

Be as Frodo.
And failing that,
Be as Sam.

July 2004

The Weft of Friends

for Duchyll

The loom of life is warped
But the weaver is blind to the pattern.
The randomness of everyday
Provides a backdrop for the colors of friendships.
Hues of emotion add subtlety and texture
To the masterwork that winds around the beam.

To maintain the tension
The strings of life are played out inch by inch.
Yesterday is but a memory and tomorrow but a dream.
The heddles rise.
The heddles fall.
The shuttle glides from side to side.

Colors come and colors go.
They enter and are played out,
Only to repeat again.
Echoes that grow sweeter with time.
Upon what other looms do they play
Lending richness and variety?

What color string do I add to the lifework of friends?
Am I the yellow of love?
Or the richness of purple?
I wish to be remembered as a rainbow
Intense and vivid
And then gone.

September 2004

The Wind Has Died

The wind has died.
The night is cold and dark.
I gaze out the window
And
A vision of myself
Appears ghostly in the glass.

Who is she?
I wonder
No longer young
Not yet old
Not wise
Foolish still
And trying to escape reality.

November 6, 2004

Grandma Memories

I hear the sounds of my grandson
Playing in his bed
Happy sounds of a contented child.

I know I should wait.
Let him enjoy
His private morning moments,
But temptation is too great
And our time together too brief.

Gently I push the door open.
I'm greeted by a glorious grin.
A bouncing boy cooing, "Hi!"
Grateful to be released from behind bars
He gives great hugs.

Safe in Grandma's arms
He travels down wooden stairs
To roughhouse on Grandma's bed.
We play, we laugh.
Squeals and giggles all around.
Unconditional love is the best breakfast.

October 2000

Seven Generations

We stand at the fulcrum of a cosmic lever
One side reaches seven generations into the past
The other, seven generations into the future.
Now is the moment of power.

It is up to us to bring the knowledge
The lessons, the experiences of our ancestors
Into the present
So that seven generations into the future
Can reap the benefits.

This is the real lesson of seven generations.
We are the link.
What we do matters.
It is true for each generation:
Now is the moment of power.

As we watch world events unfold, we pray:
Pray to heal the hurts of seven generations in the past.
They are the source of today's pain.
Pray to heal the suffering of today's events.
That there may be peace for the seventh generation to come.

April 1999

A Blessing

May this be your path:
Wrap everyone you meet
In an envelope of love
Intention and focus
Be present with each
Above all
May you find love

May your days be filled with acts of kindness
Caring for one who cares for you
Simple pleasures
Simple gifts from the heart
Expressions of love
Manifested in the present
Creating a world
For two alone

May 21, 2005

Melinda Morris Perrin considers herself a "Folk Poet", untrained and inspired by the things she sees and experiences. Melinda married her high school sweetheart in their home town of Hamburg, New York and set up residence in Schenectady. They have three children and four grandchildren.

The family moved to Chicago in 1980 where Melinda continued her work as a television producer. During that period she reawakened to the heartbeat of the Earth and began writing poetry. While in the Midwest, Ms. Perrin studied with many Native American teachers and returning to her roots in Western New York, became a teacher of the Seneca Wolf Clan Teaching Lodge and the Seneca Indian Historical Society. Ms. Perrin's first book of poetry contains writings from this time of her life. *Prairie Smoke: Writings from the Heartland* illuminates the spiritual realm of nature and its interaction with the physical.

A Plant Spirit Medicine practitioner, Ms. Perrin was a leader and spiritual healer of Prairyerth, an earth-centered spiritual Fellowship of the Unitarian Universalist Association from 1998 to 2004. She was a presenter at the Parliament of the World's Religions in Cape Town, South Africa in 1999, and the keynote speaker at the University of Iowa's Harvest Lecture Colloquium on Natural Prayer. She continues to be a frequent presenter and guest lecturer at universities, conferences and congregations of various affiliations throughout the United States. While in Chicago, she co-chaired the Living Treasures of North America Heritage Awards for four years. In 2003 she and her husband were honored in turn as "Everyday Living Treasures", Melinda for her work to honor the Elders and keep the teachings alive, and Dan for his dedication to folk music.

Ms. Perrin earned triple honors in Natural Religion, Earth Law, & Ethnobotany at Northeastern Illinois University in 2002. She was the Executive Director of the Conservation Research Institute in Elmhust, Illinois when she and her husband, Dan, moved back to Eastern New York in October of that same year.

Goldenrods: Love Poems for the Old & Foolish is her second book of poetry. It is inspired by love rediscovered and reclaimed following her husband's serious accident the day before they moved into their new home. Her poetry is included in *A Place of Your Own* by Edward Searl and she is a frequent contributor to *Whirling Rainbow* and to *Sophia,* two Unitarian publications. Many of her writings on "Coming of Age" will appear in upcoming editions from Skinner Press, edited by Rev. Ed Searl.

Similar books of interest from the Ice Cube Press—find out more at www.icecube.press.com

Prairie Smoke: Writings From the Heartland, Melinda Perrin, $8.95
Melinda Perrin's first collection of poetry. An inspiring blend of spirit and place-based poetry mixed together with words of prayer. All stemming from her background in Native American Spirituality, Ethnobotany, religion and as a Plant Spirit Medicine practitioner. These poems show a remarkable ability to be aware of the natural and social communities in which each of us live.

This Goddess Grows A Garden, Joan Riise, $11.95
"a special book which provides a unique and intimate understanding of that mystery which has made the gourd so special to humans for thousands of years. Many thanks to Joan and Lenny, and all the others who participated in this project, for sharing not only their expertise, but even more importantly, their poetry and their dreams"--Ginger Summit, author, Complete Book of Gourd Craft

Prairie Weather $10
A fascinating collection of writings on the meanings, the events and influences of our Midwestern, prairie weather. In the tradition of our harvest books this collections stems from our belief that our "environmental crisis is a crisis of our souls." As a result, we must search for manners to improve our environment requires improving our souls. Featuring new writings by Jim Heynen, Mary Swander, Robert Sayre, Amy Kolen, Scott Cawelti, Debra Marquart, Thomas Dean, Patrick Irelan and Ron Sandvik.

Living With Topsoil, $9.95

Many living in Iowa and the Midwest are residents to the richest, fertile land in the world. What does this mean in a spiritual and environmental sense? Explore this idea through writing by Mary Swander, Cornelia F. Mutel, Michael Carey, Patrick Irelan, Thomas Dean, Larry Stone, Timothy Fay and an introduction by Steve Semken.

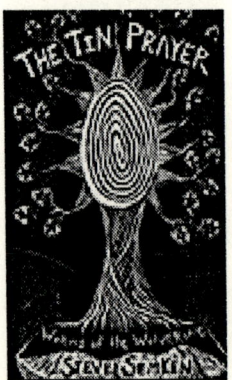

The Tin Prayer, 11.95

Written while artist-in-resident at the Island Institute in Sitka, Alaska this book is a confessionary tribute to growing up and making sense of the Midwest. "Part-memoir, part-manifesto, written with the naïve hutzpah of great folk art!"—*Little Village News*

Natural Movements, $6.95

This fascinating book explores ties between sacred geometry and the ancient form and path of the labyrinth. The book includes original prints and corresponding path diagrams with detailed descriptions making Natural Movements an easy book to learn from and read.

To order send check & mailing address to:
Ice Cube Press 205 N Front St.
North Liberty, Iowa 52317-9302
information@icecubepress.com   www.icecubepress.com

The Ice Cube Press began publishing in 1993 to focus on how to best live with the natural world. Since this time we've been recognized by a number of well known writers including Gary Snyder, Gene Logsdon, Wes Jackson & Barry Lopez. We've published a fair number of well known authors too, including Mary Swander, Jim Heynen, Paul Gruchow and many others. Check out our other books at our web site and see why we are dedicated to "hearing the other side."

Printed in the United States
37661LVS00004B/58-105